BLESSING

PRINCETON SERIES OF CONTEMPORARY POETS

For Other Books in the Series,

see p. 54

BLESSING

POEMS BY

Christopher Jane Corkery

PRINCETON UNIVERSITY PRESS

Copyright © 1985 by Princeton University Press

Published by Princeton University Press, 41 William Street,
Princeton, New Jersey 08540
In the United Kingdom: Princeton University Press, Guildford, Surrey

LIBRARY OF CONGRESS CATALOGING IN PUBLICATION DATA

Corkery, Christopher Jane, 1946–
Blessing.

(Princeton series of contemporary poets)
I. Title. II. Series.
PS3553.O6477B4   1985   811'.54   84-42879
ISBN 0-691-06631-0 (alk. paper)
ISBN 0-691-01418-3 (pbk.)

Publication of this book has been aided by a grant from the
Paul Mellon Fund of Princeton University Press

This book has been composed in Linotron Bembo

Clothbound editions of Princeton University Press books are
printed on acid-free paper, and binding materials are chosen for
strength and durability
Printed in the United States of America by Princeton
University Press, Princeton, New Jersey

Designed by Laury A. Egan

Acknowledgments

Some of the poems in this book (a few in slightly altered versions) first appeared in the following publications:

"Bestiary" in *Southern Poetry Review*

"Water" and "Metamorphosis to Punta Gorda" Copyright © 1979 by The Antioch Review, Inc. First appeared in *The Antioch Review*, Vol. 37, No. 4 (Fall, 1979). Reprinted by permission of the Editors.

"Ephraim's Reflection" (as "Barter"), "Looking for the Happy Family," and "The Curator in Love" in *Soundings/East*

"Letter from Marcellus, Maker of Fountains, to Cominia His Mother" in *Tendril*

"Orphan's Song" in *Ploughshares*

"Memento Mori" in *Harvard Magazine*

"Winter Song" in *Dear Winter* (Northwoods Press, 1984)

"February 14," "Spoken Spanish," and "Some Things a Prisoner Knew" in *Poetry*

"The Annunciation" first appeared in *Ironwood* and was reprinted in *The Pushcart Prize IX: Best of the Small Presses* (Pushcart Press, 1984)

Special thanks are due to Yaddo, to The Ingram Merrill Foundation, and to The MacDowell Colony. Their generosity and support have counted for much in the completion of this volume.

For Patrick

Contents

The Annunciation   3

The Curator in Love   4

La Señora Fernández Née Slater, the Editor's Wife, Is Gone   6

Magdalen's Song   8

Puccini Is Not Interested in Women   9

Orphan's Song   11

In a Sargasso Bottle   12

Metamorphosis to Punta Gorda   13

Roulette   16

This Island Is the Only Home We Have   18

Prayer   21

Spoken Spanish   22

Letter from Marcellus, Maker of Fountains, to Cominia
     His Mother   24

Bestiary   28

Photos at an Exhibition: Man and Boy Fishing   29

The Painter Speaks of Blue and His Beginnings   30

Grown Older, the Painter Demurs When They Ask   32

What Is Love? 'Tis Not Hereafter   33

February 14   34

What Can We Do, You Ask Me, Deprived of the Particular?   35

When the Lamp Burns Out   36

Shell   38

Ephraim's Reflection   39

Coastal History   40

Some Things a Prisoner Knew   42

Spastic   43

Winter Song   44

Divorce   45

Looking for the Happy Family   47

Memento Mori   48

The Song   50

Water   52

The Dog   53

BLESSING

The Annunciation

The angel of the Lord came unto me
carrying a dove with curious, blinking eyes.
The angel said to me in an accent I had heard
This is the spirit of the word. And then,
You are the one who shall bear it.
The words hung there, like inedible fruit,
while the angel stiffly cleared his throat.
Yet I rejoiced greatly, not knowing why,
but sensing that my pleasure,
once caught inside this room,
was suddenly boundless and that it let me see
beyond the dust in the fly-thick road
and the cankered chickens pecking at the door,
beyond my neighbor Isa whose sobs cut the air,
beyond the web of Father's swollen hands.
I am chosen? I asked again, as if I could be sure.
And the angel pointed. *See the dove? It stays.*
And indeed it had found a little perch
in the deepest slit of our one white wall.
You are blessed among women, a mellow tone now,
and all will rejoice when you bear your fruit.
The angel paused here and began to smile
and amazed, I understood, exactly, what was meant,
as if another voice were speaking inside me.
So I took the tally board that Father made for market
and the pot of nettle liquor, pulling out the cork.
Then I plucked and cleaned a quill from that quiet bird.
The angel seemed disturbed.
I began to write.

The Curator in Love

The curator has died of light
inside the Dutch room many times.
His job is to take care but he is lost
in questions that bring hazard—
about the stroke that made the light
not knowing what it meant, about the life
that enters him as deftly as a needle.
He does not know if he completes the picture
by his standing there.

Dutch or French, he thinks, the country pales
beside the other matter—what came first?
Even if all was prearranged—
six hunting still lifes for the Countess of Enghien,
the ugly little children of Wilhelm Van de Groot—
what surfaced almost never was mundane,
as if an eye could see around a corner.

Here, for example, a woman stands
beside a man who smokes an ivory pipe.
His hand is gnarled and scraped
like a mottled clot of bulbs.
Her hand touches the light
expecting more than she has life for.
And the light that comes from somewhere
that is not the smudged-in window
puts their bodies into motion,
then seals them off forever, and settles
on the tumbled sling of rabbits on the floor.

He draws closer, then draws back,
as if he could see more, as if his tongue
could do a thing but harbor in his mouth.
By mental arcs he has twirled out
to this unmental place, come to the wet
and petaled nub—body or the brush?

The crowd hums and grows uncomfortable.
They want to know what century, and why.

He draws closer, then draws back.

La Señora Fernández Née Slater, the Editor's Wife, Is Gone

He lets the garden go.
Her wild articulation
unfolds against the asphalt yard,
balsam, phlox, and loose-strife
clotting in one corner.

And in the street La Borinqueña
loses to La Habanera. Then they lose
to the Ponce Kings. Uptown,
the Cuban league's ascending in the August steam.
Papaya vendors whine a Monday tune.

And in the hall her scorebook, walking stick, straw hat.
Her gnarled pronunciation of their names is gone,
and theirs of hers, Slater turned to Slahtair.
Her steps are gone, but there are imprints in the air
that stop him.

Always, at first, apologies.
Not for death, but for shoes
around the room, books under the bed,
for his refusal to use soap.

And in the office, two mounds of paper
ground his desk, purporting to be stories.
This time, says the agent, a woman's real life
has been captured. This time, once again,
he rejects the pallid offer.

Ashes to ashes. He will accept
the one that cancels this equation.
He shouted only once, and asked her to come back.
Her shell of an ear is God's ear now,
engendering the ocean, the teams and books forgotten
in a Caribbean swell.

He waits for one that will tell him
of her wrists shrunk in the cuff,
the head growing back to childhood,
past language, and to infancy,
forgetting sin, and hair, and knowledge.
The eyes, open and complete. One day,
receiving his look like food. The next,
blank to all offers.

If one could say what absence is,
he'd take it; could see what's wilting in the Toltec cup
and know that it's called larkspur.
If one could tell him what to do
with the statue they have brought,
Nuestra Señora de la Paz
in a wreath of pink and orange.

Magdalen's Song

I am a portal. Men pass through.
No one gives me blessing.
Uncle was first, when I was twelve.
The black bees kept on humming.

When I gave Jesus food and drink
I did not say my name.
Simon would tell him later, I knew.
By then I would be gone.

I only wanted to bring him the figs,
two fat ones, just at their peak.
And a pitcher of water from Levi's well,
where only the holy walk.

I did it, and ran away through the crowd.
Simon's shouts filled the air.
But what are a fisherman's taunts to me,
or the fat little taxman's jeer?

I am a lintel, flower-hung.
Nobody knows but me.
I understand how his life ends.
Leaves. Then wind. A tree.

Puccini Is Not Interested in Women

Only this one, wings pinned to a bark.
The distance between her song
and what is happening to her
keeps him up late, and makes him thin,
sweat forming as he sees her hair disheveled,
white back moving out the door.
A hand reaches for a knife, or pen,
then throws it off, repulsed.

One way to keep a woman is to write
what he would have her say
in a book, or opera, or play.
But still, she sometime wills her way
down towards life's detritus,
rilling in a darker sea than his.

She loves a stupid navy-man
who's never been to Italy,
knows not a thing of art
or how an eggplant ripens;
knows nothing of the strain to crystallize a chord
that pulls the heart and genitals and bowels
into one nameless arc.
Knows nothing, always nothing.

One way to keep a woman is to kill her.
By her own hand, of course; it is her nature,
in the end, and not his own that bids it.
He makes her death a weightless bridge
that laces up the gap between two countries,

between suicide and happiness, between
most men and women.

The bridge soars up, countless times,
a monument to those on either side.
But he is always in between, the glint
of realness always somewhere else,
where knives are only raised in self-defense,
and dark wings pulse above the kelp-held waters,
where hair, unloosened nightly from all that held it back,
renews him in the shadow of Mount Aso.

Orphan's Song

My mother's house was made of clematis, I think.
And Clematis is what Miss White calls Mother Ghost all day.
She tells her what to clean, says, *Clematis, clean this.*
But I know Mother Ghost's her name and she made up three songs.
We sing them every Sunday when Mr. Dearing visits.

And when we put the hymnals back and pull their ribbons tight
(black goes next to red, purple next to white)
it's Mother Ghost who tells us by the way she stands
the next week has begun, and it will end.
Then Miss White says hush, and takes the light.

But Mother Ghost comes back and rubs her hand across my eyes.
I dream that all the bulls are dressed in flowers.
Their legs are wet and stamping where the steam keeps puffing up.
The sun is hiding deep inside the bulls.

In a Sargasso Bottle

Dear Diary, the letter said,
I have been made of glass.
But lately all the elements
that fixed this smooth cohesion
have undergone a vicious change,
lost their grip on wholeness.
And I am turning into things
I cannot understand,
like water on a withered stalk
bent double in the field,
or wind that cuts grooves in the bay,
craving a certain sail.

Dear Diary, you never tell me
how these words affect you.
But now you must, I am about
to suffer dissolution.
You must know how little there is left
of my polished, countable future.
What I am today is a rust-bitten spade,
the salt-lipped wail of a bell.

Metamorphosis to Punta Gorda

I.

The point is not that you would not notice.
The point is I could do it.
Every day a precipice of choice
presents itself in flattened situations.
A man, a husband of twenty-three years,
a gynecologist, walks out one morning
and, perhaps, finding in the air
the precise temperature of departure,
goes to the bus station,
embarks for Punta Gorda, and does not bother
to write, to call, to ever breathe again
into their lives.

How many times, being away from those that mattered,
have I known, without surprise,
that I could stay in this city or that town
and find, within weeks, or months,
a whole other river, a new globe of air,
and lives that matter equally?

The answer is many times.
But even so, this talent on my part
was not a thing I cherished;
rather, an aberration of the lonely,
like a sixth finger, rarely useful,
always an affront.

2.

No one here can guess the joke
of my wearing white. Everyone wears it.
Loose cotton pants and shirt
to let the sun seep through, not burn.
I am almost an obscenity standing here,
probing no one's body,
feeling no one's pulse
except the ocean's.

No one here knows me, or what my business was.
Perhaps there is a woman here, one whom I could touch.
It would be the way it was
the first time I saw snow,
having come up from Baton Rouge
to do my internship.
Not like snow, of course, but still
like that blunt firstness, naked
only the way fruit is naked,
guiltless like the porpoises
that swim here off the shore.

It will not matter in the end
that I left them so much money.
Let them talk at the clinic.
My wife, of all, will talk the least,
knowing most, and underneath her cool aversion
a bubble will be forming of compressed heat,
of heart heat, the likes of which I've never seen,
and when it surfaces her old heart will shatter,
deafening as my silence.

It does not matter now, by the water.
The truth is I will never touch a woman's breast
in passion, or any other way.
What is left is simply to dissolve,
like smoke or fog,
take on the contours of the sand,
turning dryness to a virtue.

There is an arc in the sunset
and I can only think of legs, spread.
The apex of the crotch crescendoes in my brain
and then subsides, becoming a horizon.
Now it is me whose legs are in the stirrups.
But there is no one in the room
and no one ever comes.

After the sun sets here
a red-blue light lingers
for an awfully long time.
It is hard to remember, really,
how it was first seeing snow.
It is hard to think of anything
but the water and the sand.

Roulette

This is the difficult part, he says,
knowing when to play.
And looking at the carved and lacquered ceiling
he remembers
everything about a certain place
but cannot tell—
for how absurd to say to her
it was in this town
that I first began a picture,
saw your face.

           He cannot say
how he remembers pansies,
dark square beds of purple
turning black against the stucco.
La Folie, Villa Mëtz, La Mère du Lac
were houses, where he drank tea and sat
in a big chair with wings
and wondered at the same time
as he saw the mountain shift
from pink to white, distinct,
if his father would come back,
if his mother really was
what the tall man called beautiful
before he turned around to face the water.

My mother—can he say to her,
as the ball clicks round the wheel—
was a very lonely woman
and I cannot forget
how she sat in the wicker chair
staring at the mountain.

The boats were mute white moths
against the navy of the lake
and I waited for a long time
thinking she would hold me.

You must wait till the last minute
and always play the black.
His hand upon her shoulder
looks to him like a white flag.
And the clicking sound reminds him
of something. He forgets.
But as she leans to touch her bet
he thinks it is a moth,
caught inside a jalousie,
the mountain's last light red.
The restless mind replays this way
the times the soul faltered.
The ball and wheel, perfect lovers,
turn without regret.

This Island Is the Only
Home We Have

I.

Let me dream that we move
the way angels do,
no stains of longing smeared
across our faces.
Unencumbered by gender
we would not scrape the dark
or live days caught in slow webs of regret.
Sexless, behemoth, all weather would be ours.
It seems a dream to dream
of such vast calm.

Say a man loves a woman.
Say black engenders white.
So tied to pain this coupling—
it cannot survive.
Yet Noah had a wife a million years ago
and a boat filled with cargo
all shivering and brute.
And they were outcast
upon a bitter sea,
thick dark sargassum
that hauls the spirit down.

They bickered over everything,
captive, coupled pilots.
Whether to slaughter the extra goat.
How to calm the tortoise.
Excesses, divisions, for years
it went like this. For years
they did not see the bird
God sent to set them free.

2.

In a fuchsia-colored cocktail room
the sharp wail of desire
surfaces, unbidden, from a mouth
that cannot pray.
It rises, but is lost,
for at that very minute
the tide has turned outside
and starts its push into the bay.

Most who might have heard the call
are numb to loss and store.
They do not hear the blossom rage
and break against the tree.
Beside a house, wisteria vines
confound a simple trellis.
Inside, someone cuts lemon,
puts one slice in his tea.

All of us seem orderly
until desire begins.
Even as it unravels,
we cover what we see.
And soon there is no hope,
we trust our own disguises,
perennial colonials
who will not be set free.

Except for Mrs. Waverly,
who knows no one holds title.
She cries at the clambake
and then, her calm retrieved,
steps off the second-story porch,

proscenium of wicker,
an angel heading home,
her flesh misperceived.

3.

Black-billed terns sweep and dive
along this ragged coast.
Oystercatchers mount their flights
from unseen nests in air.
But if today an angel
came flying over the island,
which of us would stand up,
which of us could leave
the struggle among bodies,
hard, sung quarrel,
and say, I see a mighty wing
repairing the torn sky?

None of us is built for it,
that blunt, unweighed departure.
Interminably we lengthen out
the cut-word of good-bye.

The wing might look like Noah's boat
or like a turtle's back.
It might look like a girl we knew,
her face etched by desire.
Yet here are no angels.
Why did I speak of angels?
Only our wingless bodies rise,
and fall, and bless the air.

Prayer

Purge this one evil: tongue that utters nothing.
Show me the word or else show me the dark
where lightning seeds its next illicit sun.
If it is love of you I haven't sung, if it is only war,
then mark me down for hiding behind doors
when Master Fear came calling. But then,
between the pearling, jointless tide I saw at dawn
and the cripple whose torqued spine breaks up this street,
teach me the connection, silent, forging one.
Shut my eyes. Pry my lips apart.

Spoken Spanish

Love is to endure, much of the time.
Endurecer, to become hard.
We become hard in this sharp weather.

It has been years since I admired
the spiny winter branches meant to shed light,
let light in. We are those spines,
their compromise with what the sun remembers.
Compromiso means appointment, the kind
you used to keep.

Endure it, this, which from the moment
it began, promised us an end, said,
absolutely silence. Whether the breath
stops because the limbs are tired
or else because a bullet fills the lungs
too full—whichever way it comes
you will persist. *Endurecer*
means become hard.

Love rains, we soak it up, then lose it
to the air, our hydrologic cycle
interrupted only, always,
by seasons that are stronger.
We call the winter *desdichado*,
because it is the wrong one.
Desdichado means unlucky,
having the wrong desire.

But when the buds come, and they do,
it is from hardened wood. That is,
madera dura, madera que persiste.
Wood which, if it could, would shrink
from such effulgence, but wood which,
at the same time, was born
to yield these blossoms.

La flor que permanece is
the flower that remains.

Letter from Marcellus, Maker of Fountains, to Cominia His Mother

A fragment, found at the villa of Cominia Flava, near
Baiae; probably written during one of the droughts
that occurred in the reign of Vespasian, 1st century, A.D.

. . . . Yes, I understand quite well. Within
two days the Senate's edict will be out,
my fountains tightly gagged. The central cistern
will be rimmed by crowds who wait in lines for what
they thought was theirs. They'll think they only mind
the wait. They will not know it is the absence
of the leap enfeebles them and queers their dreams
at night. The surge the spirit needs to live
is gone without the fountains. Soon in a rush
they'll all convert to that Judaean god
who marks his own with water.

                                        You say you fear
that I have made an idol out of fountains.
And if I have? What is the danger there?
What can I do, in any case, but praise
the thing that freed me? My own conversion came
so long ago (to fountains, Mother, not the Jew)
that I must be their high priest. But I can live
without them, for a month at least. My self
has been imparted to the air so many times
that everywhere I look I see a sign
of water.

            Remember, Mother, down at Ostia,
close beside the sea? That was the first,
that fountain made of stones that they had shaped
into a dolphin. The black glass eyes

reflected me, at twelve, two years without
my hearing or my speech. But I could see
the sound inside his eyes, the water flowing
past them. I had begun to read the tiny
movements in your own each time I saw you
watch me.

That day around your neck you wore
the gold, Etruscan dolphin Quintus gave you.
You have it still, I think. But it was crude
and bore no link to water. The fountain dolphin
arched his back and spewed the water out
for hours. He was too small. It never got him
closer to the sea.

And then when your next
husband Lucius took us to Judaea, we saw
those fountains in the desert, not built
but venerated. Remember the dark men?
(I know you do, you watched them.) Each day
they moved the piles of rocks and lined the rows
with skins, a fevered effort meant to catch
however much they could when chaos happened.
At dusk the sand would split and some dark force
they had no name for shot the water out
and up a hundred hands.

After it fell
our party moved around the rocks, admired
the makeshift leather gutters and how the water
ran into a circle, then a well. But I
was more concerned, and am, with why
the water heaved up from its source,

choosing to leave that solace. From then
I wanted only to imagine that I could know
what water's purpose was.

I knew then
that my fountains would be what words had been.
They would reiterate the way that all lost things
come back, the way that tongues and openings
rise up in nameless places.

But you, Mother,
find all of this detail. Year after year
you send me oily seers from the East
who say that they can loose my speech, and then
explode a box next to my ears. Fearful
for the gold that they might lose, they blame
the birds or else the augurer, mouthing
with their rotten mouths, "Oh excellent
Marcellus!"

You had to bear
my sickness, Mother, and then the aftermath.
But you have never healed yourself, as I have.
You only see the blighted child, you look down
in dismay. Ignoring what I've done
you send in cures for what's no longer
a disease—it is my life.
And if the fountains lured me, how much more
they've given back (let us be frank)
than if I had relied upon your remedies,
or husbands, or childish hope of speech.

Mother, do not concern yourself, for me
or for this edict. Already twice today
I've walked around the city. The fountains
seem more full, more white, than ever
I have seen them, and rising with a sound
that even I can hear. It is a sound
that Ostian dolphin would have bellowed to the air
if I had had the muscle to release him.
It is a sound my father would have laughed to hear.

But I must store this all away, save it
for what's coming. Mother, my greetings to your
husband. They say he wears his youth well.

And Mother, I salute you.

Bestiary

Pigs and chickens also stumble in the dark,
make wrong decisions, eat a rotten kernel,
come to the dawn to find no garbage waiting.

Or I can tell you of roots and trees, bougainvillea
trailing, hibiscus growing up without precision,
dams where beavers build and unbuild,
allowing leaks to seep, not waiting
for our praise. Beauty unbuckles in the night
in places where you'd least expect it.

An endless process of translation, us
to the bestiary and back. But heart
is spoken here in every language:
chicken, pig, hibiscus, bougainvillea, beaver.
Sometimes it's too much to bear,
tails slap the water hard, or curl up
in the snuffled air; someone scratches
for feed, then stops and stands on one leg,
listening.

Photos at an Exhibition:
Man and Boy Fishing

Except, man stares out
at grey lake, grey eyes intent
and brutish as the water.

Boy's eyes (round boy, of umber)
regard that timeless watcher
which shamelessly records

what never was intended to be shown,
the battle in the boy, of voices,
one side saying "Fishing!" and,

"My father caught . . . ," the other
crying out, oracular:
"Cast up, what good my silver coat

in gasping, greying, neuter death,
an end that I have not deserved
for my supposed intrusion into air."

Except, the picture takes no step
beyond the stare; the eyes are yours
that round off the connection.

The Painter Speaks of Blue
and His Beginnings

I.

If I call it Homeric
you will take me literally.
Try to understand this, just as the sky
meets water in your eye, and in the fact
of their atoms, there always is one point
where the picture stops, even though
you feel the water bobble.

2.

I have pursued the clear space
that lies between two people,
unbreachable by will. It has nothing to do
with fruit or clouds. It is a whole,
silent cloth. I leave it to you
to classify the colors.

3.

The moments I remember are by water.
Ambiguity seemed pointless and shapes
made gender quite irrelevant. I learned blue,
and what October meant, and that my father
always would go free.

4.

I wanted to trade him for the ocean
but he refused to go. Now that I am older
I use a pale haze. Inevitably
they take this for emotion.

5.

Yes, I still pursue that color.
No, I am not gloomy.
This is not a dried-up well or cave.
Water and air abound. People move.
Light converges constantly
with what is not light.
I try to paint the echo.

Grown Older, the Painter Demurs
When They Ask

I have said all I could
about pictures and language.
And there is no word
for what the colors do.
What we do in words
can only defeat us
if we try to think of color,
equating the two.
I will not even speak
of the pictures you have brought me.
I would be mad to try,
to articulate the green.
But I will sit and face them
and wait until my eyes
record every side
of the colors' conversation.
I cannot say more.
Pictures or language?
I cannot even tell you
why my hands shake today.
I will place my body quietly.
I will not ask you anything.
My skin will absorb now
what the pictures say.

What Is Love?
'Tis Not Hereafter

Not now, either, but back, and in between.
And if I move on brick or asphalt roads,
on dust, or good intentions, or concrete,
do not fault me for always looking back.
I need to know what place this is before me,
what antique clock undoes the present hour.

Perhaps this very hour, September, noon,
with sentience caught between a smell of apples
and the obtuse insistence of a hammer.
And if tomorrow's what I've said I long for—
my future, my release from order—I renounce the ruse.

It is a girl whose dress constrains her body.
She lived a hundred years ago, lives still.
She sits at a piano, studying her hands.
An apple lies discarded on the sill.

Outside her house a wagon rolls by, slowly.
Whatever the horse hauls, she doesn't need.
Erect at first, her body mirrors prefatory scales,
then sways into sonata. Place recedes.

The past can change its shape as fast as music.
Whichever face it wears, its breath is fast.
The girl, the house, the horse in its dark labor,
all shift behind me, closer, straining measure.

I keep on moving, too, until they catch me—
and they will—the song her fingers offer
finally heard.

February 14

Various people will tell you
All about love, about poems. But
Listen, nobody ever can say how
Endless the love of words is.
Nightly and daily, words and love
Trip over each other, combine, find
In each other what *possible* means:
No word is meant to live by itself.
Each one looks for a listener.

What Can We Do, You Ask Me, Deprived of the Particular

If I do not describe a Persian miniature,
the painted flame no bigger than a flea,
what can I tell you?
If I do not present you with a pail full of cold water
or a basin blue with bulbs,
what can I show you
to let you know I live?

More than all the single things I'd name—
a list that I have loved as well as you—
more than all that matters.
It is the colorless procession gone before,
the mind and thought entwined on their one journey.
And if they only shuffle, towards something out of sight,
there is a grace in what occurs,
high stars shedding light,
the smallest shape conceiving
its own edges over time.

Whatever gifts you bring me
I bow in admiration,
but less for what you carry
than the longing at its core.
No flame or jagged tulip
ascends without that heat.
They rise and blush as children
of the mind's persistent offer.

When the Lamp Burns Out

The girl has left the parlor,
left them in the light.
Hers is a world where walls fall down,
deep in the pitch of dreams.

And there she sees her mother
touching death's wood gate.
She sees her father's hands at rest
and the light slips past his linen cuffs
to settle on his fingers.

And though her father's eyes are closed
she knows that he can see,
that he reviews the spiral path
of the road that was his life
and at the end the bright light it released.

Her mother's eyes see nothing, first,
in this sleep that is the girl's,
but then a pair of newborn lambs
emerge out of the dark.
Their burnished hooves are wet
and glimmer like her patent shoes.

Pressed from the perfect circle
they stumble towards the lamp,
looking for heat, not knowing what light means.
But something licks their lids apart,
though they would keep them shut,
before the dark place vanishes completely.

When the lamp burns out, the girl knows,
the parents fall away.
And she knows that then her fingers
will become encyclopedic.
They will touch the springless armchairs
and the mirror's beveled edge.

They will find the trestle table
and the half-door in the kitchen.
They will trace the outlines of the shed,
of each post in the gate,
and clutch the thickened, greasy coats
of the hard old ram and ewe.

But now she waits, her fingers limp,
at rest against the sheets.
The sweet and sightless core
is what surrounds her like a light,
and she dreams that all are innocent
until the lamp burns out.

Shell

All things sustain me,
even the dream of rivers.

Though I cannot thrive bereft of salt,
I still can understand the heave down to the delta.

All comes together there—rain, tide, and seed.
Three sides shaping one wide mouth—mother, father, daughter.

But I was made in steeper places.
Harsher barrens nursed me.

To have seen not far away the skein of the great baleen
is to believe in measure, and also, in dying.

Yet my song has a long life: *aqua   mare   pax*.
My song lifts and plummets: water   ocean   peace.

Ephraim's Reflection

I don't expect them back,
these children who have rolled away
out of my sight and hand,
like pennies I dropped long ago,
thought not worth retrieving.

Now copper seems the warmest color;
small number, one, the best and only.
One is what they asked to be,
individual, not like another,
or like enough, but not the same.
I have spent too many years engaged in barter,
imagining only struggle
could yield up resolution.

Now I sit quiet,
feel the light unfolding.
Waiting for the sun to cover me
in copper, I shine,
as if surrounded by children.

Coastal History

An empty concrete parking lot
beside an Italian restaurant,
and that formica palace
itself beside the water.

New England in October
and three brown pairs of heels
add their muffled echoes
to the distant call of geese.

A girl walks between her parents.
Everything is blue.
Italy looks like a shoe.
She thinks her hands are angels.

Who can be blamed for abstraction
when love comes down to this?
Just blue-gold air their bodies break
as they cross the lot to home,

and far out on the water,
something flying, gone.

1982
October still. New England's older.
Birds hold up the air.
No one from Siena escorts her on the sand.
Nothing happens as her mother promised.

Inside, one waiter mops the floor,
following her last order.
Clumps of papery, garlic stars
stud the plastic arbor.

Not at the sight of homing geese
does she lift up her head,
but rather at their leader's cry,
his most unphysical fall.

That sharpened lust for harbor
explains her whole life well.
She blesses God, holds herself,
then bends to touch the water.

Some Things a Prisoner Knew

That butter comes from cows, and margarine
was foisted on the Turks. That certain dogs
circle a bed four times on hearing thunder.
That monarch butterflies taste bad, and bridges
(seen historically) fall more than they stand.

My brother never meant to steal. The company
planned it all. They never intended
to give him the land. They meant to go in with rifles.

How can I say that one life holds a future?
How can I say that other lives are dross?
If I remembered everything that happened
and laid it out just like this pack of cards,
you'd still be looking underneath to find a darker story.
You can't believe that King protects his Jack.

Spastic

He rolls and lurches
as if every air that blew
could tilt his body back and forth,
raise his arms like sails.

The unrefusable hurricane
awash inside his brain
spends itself in a stammering spine,
foils him in each bone.

But see, this apparition
has a mortal mother.
She comes: round, plaid, a prow,
sixty to his forty.

Entering the Rialto
they surge up like a ship
whose bow can break whatever weather
man or god could rage.

I stand on the corner
a few minutes longer
while the air says something.
The buckled day heaves.

I reach for words but none stand.
The best careen and founder.
I wonder what are blessings,
who will take me home?

Winter Song

Rain drips down, from trees to hedge,
and last week's snow wears a grey disguise.
The cold has chiseled our breath to an edge
that wounds each song, till it falls and dies.

In the white kitchen, someone uncovers
a plate of cold stew. Nothing much
but that to eat, and a pound of liver
that says For Kitty Do Not Touch.

A shutter bangs against the house.
It keeps on banging as if someone
thought that a small, persistent abuse
could prove him right, right his wrongs.

Yet out in the abandoned garden
nothing stirs that might rescind
the rigors of its gnarled position,
once made supple by two gloved hands.

And the house's windows, eyes of ice,
fix their stare on the childless snow.
What will undo this wretched stasis?
When will spring let the wild seed go?

Divorce

A small girl on a porch
left by her mother
while Mother drives Father
to the 8:02 train.

Father always goes
when the sun hits the porch.
It is June, those are lilacs,
she does not know the word

for what is hers,
what is his.
What is the thing
between them?

But she does feel something
pressing against her
as the Plymouths and Fords
bump along the road.

It is flying inside her,
trying to get out.
It is rising through her body,
beating in her hands.

She feels tears in her eyes
but they are not hers.
They belong to those stupid
girls in the stories.

Her legs are crossed
at the ankles. Her feet swing
above the grey boards
where six ants are running.

She knows that the birds
in the lilacs are warblers.
Her father told her that
but flicker is her favorite

word for a bird.
The white on his back
when he flies away
is how she remembers.

Flicker. Flicker.

The red on his head
means love forever.
He's a good bird, she says.
And he loves to fly.

Looking for the Happy Family

The laughing picnic group, low tide in the distance,
a sea-washed pier, yellow light descending;
someone waves a chicken leg at the photographer,
grit on the lens, a lost key shining in the sand.

And then the other ones, some posed, some not,
all candids of survival, love drowning
in a contest of endurance. Except for one
or two: a man descending from a DC-3, waving,
Panama hat pushed back on his head, tan suit
floating on a thin body; he looks for all the world
as though he doesn't have a family.

Mostly I complain that in none of them
have I seen a face that dreams of dolphins,
a body tired from loving, a mind worn thin
for a bad song. I want to strip them naked,
haul in the tide, hang up the moon.
I will demand to know what happened,
and how I was bequeathed to life.
They stare back noncommittal, perhaps
a glimmer of reproach.

The hands, though, offer something, as they sit
on laps or wave, or hold a metal railing or hover
by a side. Some, if you look closely, say:
I am dying. Some say, I will survive. They say,
will he never come, the lover I've imagined?
Or else they say, for other eyes,
we put on other clothing.

Memento Mori

Death has come here only once.
It couldn't have been quicker.
It took my husband's father, left
its thumbprint on my shoulder.

Death has come just that one time,
with a watery, slipping step.
But its hands are huge, its grip a vise.
I know it will come back.

Death has come here quite enough.
When it comes again
I'll refuse to talk at all,
I'll cover my arms and then

Death will begin in a breezy voice.
The bruise will disappear.
And all the men I could never reach
will whisper in my ear.

Their words will be *yours* and *listen*,
their words will be *always calm*,
as each one tells me Death lives well,
that I can't survive the storm,

that failure is over, war's asleep,
the bottle it held is empty.
But something shines in the sun, half-clear.
Death's vessel is never empty.

I didn't know Death the first time.
But I'll know it when it comes back.
I'll know the eight boats with amethyst sails.
I'll know the pale crew in black.

The tattoo blooms on my shoulder,
though I hide it from common view.
Yet everyone's body swims in Death's swell.
Why should it spare me, or you?

The Song

For Tom

Late one night they make a baby.
It's fall and nobody cares about birth.
The men with briefcases on the train
read about trenches as they go rocking.
Yet nobody really mentions death,
and the night is far too wet for flame.

It never takes an obvious flame
to make the seed that becomes a baby.
And babies don't give a hoot about death.
They can't even say the word for birth.
All they want is sucking and rocking,
a breast, or a lap, or a choo-choo train.

No matter how hard, you can't stop the train
that hurtles out of the tunnel where flame
and blind desire are the start of that rocking,
those long dark lunges that push out the baby
to lights and the grinning faces of birth.
But the baby can't tell it a bit from death.

No one goes through that fast dark death,
that slamming, tunneling, slippery train,
with any intention, no knowledge of birth-
day cakes or snappers or pink candle flame.
All that lights up the mind of the baby
is dreams of the dark where water was rocking.

Soon baby in mother's arms goes rocking,
forgets every little thing about death.
And she sings to it, *Lullaby little baby,*
I'll get you a bright blue wooden train
and a white little sheep, and the candle flame
on your cake will show, each year, that your birth

was the grandest, most magnificent birth!
And on your sixth we'll give you a rocking-
horse with a saddle the color of flame.
And there won't be any time for death,
and later there'll be an electric train
(which would be too much for a little baby).

So love's hard flame is the only death
she sings, and it's just like birth, the rocking,
the shoot's green train, the blossom, the baby.

Water

We cannot be as water always.
Cannot fall graceful
over treacherous rocks
continuous to the pool below,
always heading home, always
having arrived there, no space
between the changes and the self.

I want to ask the child who tunnels
up from your dim past:
your eyes, how did you come by them
that trace the lineaments of love
in the remotest longing?
Your ears that hear the sound
of footfall far away
intimating oh what is it
coming soon to round the corners of your blood?
Your hands that tell me what the child could not,
how did you find them in that deafmute's country?

We cannot be as water always
but only on occasion,
the graceless hands turned up,
revealing grace, the tongue
once mute, released,
and yielding for a moment
what the heart had always felt.

The Dog

The dog with the bleeding side is yours and mine.
It roams in valleys stretched across the sky.
It never asks for pity, it is not
concerned with pity, or with useless thought.

The dog with the bleeding side patrols the earth.
Its power rains on everything that hurts.
From its wound pours a stunning, soothing balm.
The child that cried, forgotten, becomes calm.

The woman beaten more than she remembers
stops to regard a star, then thinks of embers
from a childhood camp. Her soul retreats.
She finds the will to leave what makes her weep.

And if such myth could cure all war-sick men
I'd shout it louder: let the she-dog in.
But what myth bows to pallid wills like mine?
I crack the night-door, watch the wild dog shine.

Who would permit such icy fangs to eat
of any human food? We like our meat,
but quiet on the bone, not like this frenzied
cur who spans the sky till wars have ended.

Where is the dog in daylight? Where at dawn?
Such questions go unanswered, and are wrong.
The dog with the bleeding side outruns the earth,
gravid with love, and meaning to give birth.

Princeton Series of Contemporary Poets

OTHER BOOKS IN THE SERIES

Returning Your Call, by Leonard Nathan
Sadness And Happiness, by Robert Pinsky
Burn Down the Icons, by Grace Schulman
Reservations, by James Richardson
The Double Witness, by Ben Belitt
Night Talk and Other Poems, by Richard Pevear
Listeners at the Breathing Place, by Gary Miranda
The Power to Change Geography, by Diana Ó Hehir
An Explanation of America, by Robert Pinsky
Signs and Wonders, by Carl Dennis
Walking Four Ways in the Wind, by John Allman
Hybrids of Plants and of Ghosts, by Jorie Graham
Movable Islands, by Debora Greger
Yellow Stars and Ice, by Susan Stewart
The Expectations of Light, by Pattiann Rogers
A Woman Under the Surface, by Alicia Ostriker
Visiting Rites, by Phyllis Janowitz
An Apology for Loving the Old Hymns, by Jordan Smith
Erosion, by Jorie Graham
Grace Period, by Gary Miranda
In the Absence of Horses, by Vicki Hearne
Whinny Moor Crossing, by Judith Moffett
The Late Wisconsin Spring, by John Koethe
A Drink at the Mirage, by Michael Rosen